TELL THE
TRUTH

TELL THE TRUTH

HENRY EDWARD GOODLOE

PALMETTO

P U B L I S H I N G

Charleston, SC

www.PalmettoPublishing.com

Paperback ISBN: 979-8-8229-3507-5

Part One

Sit back and relax. Let me talk about a place called the United States of America—a place that was built up and got its richness on the backs of slaves, from *their* blood, sweat, tears, and heartbreak for no pay, and later from black people's for a little pay, and the white man profited from it all. And some white people have the balls to say reparation should not be paid to black people because slavery was so long ago. If black people are not due reparations for slavery part one, we damn sure are due reparation for slavery part two, which began in 1865, the same year that slavery part one ended. Some white people say black history should not be taught in school—my guess is they don't want people to know the truth about how sinful slavery was, or they might be afraid it will be known that their ancestors owned slaves, and that's how they got their riches.

There is a love train coming, and everybody who doesn't get on board is going to be left behind like the people Noah left behind when the flood came. He tried to warn them, but they just kept on partying. Noah might have been someone like me: poor, uneducated, someone some people might call a nobody. But I've studied black people for nine years in Arkansas, Texas, and Tennessee, and I've found that black people suffer from an *illness* that's called anger. The anger comes from how badly our African ancestors were treated as slaves, and this anger is passed down from generation to generation. Just like any other illness, the longer it goes without treatment, the worse it gets. I notice every generation getting more angry and less tolerant, and white people have a condition too, called hate, that also began in slavery and is taught from generation to generation.

Let me give you an example. When I lived in Texas, I was on the walking trail, and when I got through walking, I sat down to cool off. This white man, woman, and two little girls were walking by. One girl looked to be about five, the other about three. When they got even with me, the girl that looked to be three pointed at me and said, "Momma, is that a nigger setting there?" My question is where a child that young learned what a so-called nigger was supposed to look like. I said to myself, "She's going to be old enough to start school soon, and she is going to call one of her black classmates a nigger, and they will teach her not to use that word again!" It's like what this one white guy I knew said: when schools integrated, he and this black guy got to fighting because he called this black guy a nigger, and he said that guy tackled him, and when he finally let him go, he taught him never to use that word again.

I don't understand why black people get mad at the words "nigger" and "colored people" and not at "African American" or "people of color." To me, calling a full race of American citizens *African* American and people of color is just as offensive as calling them nigger. If we are called what we are, black, *maybe* people will treat us just as American citizens, not people of color or African Americans. Some people might like to call us African American because they don't think we are full-blooded Americans. Anyway, how come white people who are born in Africa and become American citizens are not called African American?

I lived on the rough side of the track, and the white man tried to hold me back. But I don't blame Trump for anything grown people say or do. They're *supposed* to know right from wrong. The Republicans love Trump now, but as soon as he falls from grace, they are going to run from him like roaches running behind the refrigerator or under the stove when you turn the light on. For Trump, it's going to be like being out on the ocean in a boat with a hole in it and no life jacket, and you can't swim. Everybody loves a winner, but when you lose, you lose alone.

President Biden did the right thing bringing the troops home from Afghanistan. The United States had no reason for being over there in the first place. If I remember correctly, the U.S. helped Afghanistan when the Soviet Union invaded in the eighties. That money the United States spent in Afghanistan could have been used to make sure every U.S. citizen had health insurance and pay black people reparations for how hard we worked our asses off for the richness of this country for no or little pay. Every politician should read this so they would think twice before they invaded another country. If the U.S. would leave these countries alone, some of them would self-destruct like the Soviet Union did after they invaded Afghanistan. They were one nation, but when the war was over, the Soviet Union broke up into twenty-six nations. It looks like the U.S. didn't learn anything from the Vietnam War.

I believe half of the people in the United States are losing their minds or have already lost them, and the other half don't give a damn. Like me, I done lost half of my mind on one side, and I don't give a damn on the other side. This one old man told me he can do the same thing to a woman now that he could do when he was twenty-one years old, but then this young guy told him what he probably had been doing with a woman all his life—use your imagination. This old man got fighting mad, so this youngster must have been right: if he had been wrong, this old man wouldn't have gotten that mad. What he said probably was a slip of the tongue; he probably just had a few drinks.

Democrats, let that election in Virginia be a wake-up call for you all. You better take care of us— the black people, the people who keep voting for you and helping save this country from destruction. If the Republicans keep winning and take charge of this country, the way they are behaving, they might send this country to hell in a handbasket—and some of us with it. In my opinion, to anybody who has a job where wearing a mask or getting the vaccination is a requirement: instead of raising hell or giving that disease to somebody else, do like I did when I was working. If I had a job and didn't like the rules, I would quit and find another job. If you cannot find a job you like, walk out into the Detroit River or some other river and don't come back.

Don't worry; be happy. Life is too short to have sorrow—you are here today and might be gone tomorrow. I feel great even when I feel down-and-out, and I don't sing a song to make me feel better. I sang a song that made me feel better. Once my Momma was working at this nursing home, and this white lady patient smacked Momma, and Momma smacked her back. This lady began to cry and told the nurse that Momma smacked her. Momma's co-workers said, "Jo is going to get fired for smacking that white woman." Momma's name was Josiephine, but everybody called her Jo. The nurse told Momma, "Miss whatever-her-name-was said you smacked her." Momma said, "Yes, she smacked me, and I smacked her back." Then the nurse told this lady patient, "You don't smack people!" Momma kept her job. Momma's coworkers respected Momma for that one thing about her. She would respect you, and she didn't care if you were black, white, man, woman, boy, or girl, but she *wouldn't* take no shit from you. If a child spit on her, she would spit back on them; if they would bite her, she would bite back. Whatever they did to her, they didn't do it but once.

If a mother raises her children the right way, they will follow that for the rest of their lives. On the other hand, if she spoils one of them, that will follow them for the rest of their life. I know a family where the mother spoiled one of her children, and he gave his mother more heartbreak than all of the rest of the children combined. If his mother would ask him to do something and he didn't want to do it, he just wouldn't do it, and the mother would make one of the other children do it. When this guy got grown, he was going with another man's wife, and the man found out about it and whipped this spoiled guy's ass. But then he got a gun and killed this woman's husband, just like all the other bad things he had been getting away with all his life.

One Christmas Eve, this lady was looking for some walnuts and pecans for Christmas. She went in this store and asked the owner if he had any nuts, and the owner said, "The last time I checked, I did!" Everybody in the store began to laugh, and this lady got mad and walked out of the store, where there was this little dog walking the streets. There was a big dog in the yard behind a fence with a closed gate. Every day, this little dog would go by there barking at this big dog, all up on the fence, barking like he wanted to get to this big dog. One day this little dog went by there, barking all up the fence as usual, but this big dog came out of the yard and tore that little dog's ass up. When he let that little dog go, that little dog said, "Who in hell left that damn gate open?" One year this black guy was looking for some mistletoe, but he didn't know the real name, so he asked for some niggertoes, the name the white man gave them. When I was growing up, if somebody would do something bad, the older people would say, "Didn't nobody make them do that but the devil." One day this guy was going to church, and when he got to church, the devil was sitting on the church steps, crying. This guy asked him why he was crying, and the devil said, "I am not doing everything people accuse me of!" People done got so bad they got the devil going to church—God have mercy on us all.

One day in church, this little boy smacked his mother so hard she began to cry. My Momma called that boy to come to her, and everybody thought Momma was going to tell him he shouldn't smack his mother. Instead, Momma told that boy, "Smack her again!" One lady said, "Miss Jo, you shouldn't tell that boy that!" Momma said, "If she's crazy enough to let him smack her and get away with it, I want to see him smack her again!" That same little boy once told this man, "I should smack them glasses off your face." His grandmother told this boy not to do that, but the man told the grandmother, "You don't have to tell him that. Let him do it." But I can't repeat what he said he would do to that boy if he did.

I hear some people say Democrats and Republicans need to reach out to each other and talk to each other more. What I've noticed is that talking to some of those Republicans makes about as much sense as me talking to myself or someone talking to an ashtray, asking it why they can't stop smoking. A few Democrats are just as bad. I've been mailing and emailing politicians for about twenty-plus years. I ask them questions, but I have never gotten a direct answer to any question. If I ask them when black people are going to get reparations for slavery, they talk about how bad slavery was and how it never should have happened and how bad black people have been treated for hundreds of years, but they don't answer my question about reparations. My question is: Do they go to school to learn how to do that, or do they learn it on the job? I probably won't ever get an answer to this question from any of them either. And the beat goes on.

I heard that this one preacher told women not to wear pants to church. My guess is he wanted them to wear them short dresses and skirts so while he's high up preaching, he can try to see under them. The only history some white people want taught in school is white history, and some of it might be wrong. Like when Columbus discovered America, they don't tell you that a black man was the navigator on the ship. Some white people are worried about how teaching black history will make some white children feel like second-class citizens. Well, how do you think black children felt during slavery when they were sold like animals and would never see their other family members again? That was worse than black history.

A fair warning to the white man whose ancestors owned slaves: for how bad some of you have treated black people all your life, you need to make amends to black people for the pain you inflicted upon them. If the Catholic church owned slaves, like I heard they did, they are also in debt to black people. If there are some black Catholics, that includes you too because you belong to the organization. If any black people's ancestors owned slaves, this includes you too. The only way their souls and your soul can be saved is if you make amends to black people for the sin brought upon them and you for owning some of God's children and for the sin you brought upon yourself. If I am wrong for thinking that way, I ask God, in Jesus's name, to forgive me. If black people get reparations, it would benefit the white people more too because everything black people need, one way or the other, we got to buy it from the white people. But still, they would rather spend the money on a useless war that don't concern them than see black people get that money. The sad thing about it is that those politicians know if black people got the money to spend, the economy would boom. I believe they don't care about the economy as long as they are living like fat rats in a cheese factory. They probably say the hell with everybody else, and life goes on.

I wish people would stop saying these singers and athletes are other people's children's role models. The only role model children have is their parents, who have stopped raising their children and now depend on other people to raise them. The reason I say this is that if somebody else's child tried to be like a singer or an athlete and make the kind of money they make and didn't succeed, that might screw up their mind and make them try to get the money an illegal way and end up in prison or dead. What I am writing comes from the head and heart. If people ask me if I am a Christian, I say I don't know the definition of a Christian. Just because a person goes to church every Sunday and gives money to the preacher and says amen and claps their hands when he preaches, does that make them a Christian? When a person reads the Bible and preaches it, do they really understand it?

Some people can't understand why the politicians in Washington can't get anything done. One reason is that there are too many people trying to make decisions. Like a few years ago, they debated for two weeks before they decided where to sign a check. There's enough people up there to make a Ten Commandments movie! People talk about more gun laws, but guns are not the problem. The only people gun laws affect are people who obey the law. Guns save lives. If a person has got hate in their heart and wants to kill, they will find a way. The person who killed the people in that federal building, he didn't have a gun. The people responsible for 9/11 didn't have a gun. OK, get all the guns off the streets, but what's next? Stop making fertilizer and gas because people use these things to make bombs that kill people?

When I was writing letters to the newspaper, some of the things I said made some white people ask me if I was mad at white people. I said no. If I was going to get mad, it would have been before the civil rights bill passed, but I am still disappointed that some white people act like black people should thank them for letting us live in the United States, when in fact they should thank black people for what we did to make the United States the great country it is. I have not heard one white person say they are sorry for slavery or for how badly black people have been treated for over four hundred years. One white person told me black people should be happy we got one month to celebrate black history. Big deal: white people have eleven months to celebrate their history! With what black people have been through, we should have thirteen months a year to celebrate black history! I also heard a white guy say black people should be happy we elected a black president, but he also said his main job was to make sure he didn't win a second time. The one black president we had, some white people treated him like he had 666 or two horns on his forehead.

I found out something about some white people: they have a hard time listening when a black person is talking. I was talking to this white guy about black people, and he took over the conversation like he knew more about black people than I do. At the time, I had been black for seventy-eight years.

It looks like some of these politicians care more about the civil rights of peoples in other countries than they do about the people in the United States. Like this one immigrant guy I worked with at General Motors, the day he retired, he said he had worked for General Motors for thirty years and had not paid one cent of federal income tax. He told me the people who run this country are crazy for letting them come over here and work tax-free while making us pay taxes. He said they are the ones who should be paying taxes, and that was funny to him. He said he was going back to his country, where he can get three dollars for his work.

Some people say when these athletes were kneeling during the national anthem, that was disrespectful to the American flag. As far as we know, they were praying—God knows we need it. My question is this: If the American flag really represents black people, why is it red, white, and blue instead of red, white, and black? When people ask me how I can write so well if I'm not educated, I say I graduated from the university of life, plus I got a Webster's dictionary for the words I can't spell. Don't get me wrong: get the best education you can, but when you do, use common sense with it. If you don't, it can be your worst enemy. If you think I am lying, what about the people the judge gave two hundred-plus years in prison? Common sense would have told them that sooner or later, those people would miss their money.

Black people, please stop killing each other. Maybe then the police will stop killing us. They probably say, "If black people don't care about killing each other, why should we care about killing them?" For example, I knew a woman who was going with this other woman's husband. I told her she should be ashamed for going with this woman's husband, and she said if the woman's husband wasn't ashamed, why should she be ashamed? Eventually this other woman found out her husband was going with this woman I knew, and she divorced him. Then this woman he was cheating with dumped him too and said she didn't want him. If he cheated on his wife with her, he would cheat on her with another woman.

It used to be, "If you want to hear a politician complain, cook a chicken and give him the wing; if you want to hear a politician lie, cook a chicken and give him the thigh." Now they do both, just for the hell of it. Ben Carson didn't have any idea why Trump put him in charge of houses, but Trump just wanted a black person to call his house nigger. Some people might get angry at me for saying that, but before you do, think about this: Carson is a doctor. If Trump cared anything about black people, he could have made Carson Surgeon General. In my opinion, abortion isn't a religious or political concern. What a woman does with her body is between her and her God.

I guess these Asian Americans see now what black people have been going through for four-hundred-plus years. Welcome to the club—it's not a good club to belong to. I was at Walmart one day, at the customer service window, and all at once I got hot and began to sweat. I looked to my right, and there was a stalk of cotton in a shopping cart. I can be driving down the highway and see a cotton field, and I get hot and begin to sweat. This woman asked me, why wasn't I married, and didn't I need someone to cook for me? I said, "No, I got a slow cooker to cook for me, and it don't talk back." Some of these politicians complain about raising the debt ceiling, but I never heard any of them complain when they got a pay raise. Some of them get paid more than they are worth anyway. If each one of them would take a 10 percent cut in pay, they would not need to raise the debt ceiling.

I had two preachers tell me that God said to obey your slave master. My question is, did God say that, or did the white man say that to try to control the slaves because he knew the slaves were very religious? If I am wrong for saying that, I ask God to forgive me. The white man has changed a bunch of things, like how Sunday used to be the last day of the week, but then somebody made it the first day of the week. A message to Republicans: keep up the good work! All these new voting laws you are making are going to backfire on you because it is going to hurt the people that vote for you the most. Democrat voters have more patience than Republican voters. You are trying to discourage black people from voting, but we've been beating the odds for over four hundred years. I heard a state passed a law making it illegal to give people food or water while they are in line waiting to vote. But a sense of humor says, Give a soul brother a bottle of wine and promise him another bottle when he votes—brother man can stand in line all day drinking his wine, talking shit, and waiting to vote. He don't need no water or food.

I remember back in the days when black people would plant a garden, and when potatoes and whatever else began to come up, the white people would dress up in their sheets and hoods and get on horses and ride through the garden and destroy everything. They didn't care that when the crop was harvested, the black people would give them some. The only reason was that they didn't like to see the black man doing better than them. I remember back in the fifties, we lived back in the country. These white folks would dress up in their sheets and hoods and ride around. They had black people afraid, and everybody thought they were back. Then black people called them haunts, and everybody found out who they were. One night this black guy was out in the woods, hunting, and these people came riding by on their horses, and this black guy shot one of them with a shotgun. This guy almost died, and that was the end of that.

I can't understand how some people can be afraid of a person who used to be their president. I can understand why I was afraid of white people when I was growing up: I was a black child, and I didn't know any better, but these people are white and grown—what's their excuse? When I was chopping and picking cotton, there were some white people poorer then me. I always wondered why they weren't doing the same thing. My guess is they were on welfare, something black people didn't know about back then. All they gave black people was some hard-ass cheese that would stop you up if you ate too much. I hear some people say black people are lazy and welfare cases. According to what I heard, there are more white people on welfare than black people. Give up, Republicans, and stop trying to get rid of Obamacare. Another example of how the white man hates to be outdone by a black person is that if a white person had gotten that insurance bill passed, everything would be OK. That goes to show that those Republicans don't care about the people that vote for them. If Obamacare goes away, that would hurt their people the most. I was watching TV one day, and this white woman said, "It's bad to be poor, but it's twice as bad to be white and poor," like it's not too bad to be black and poor. Another time I was watching TV, this white woman said, "I like Obamacare, but I am still going to vote for the Republicans." The reason they vote for the Republicans is that they know the Democrats are going to bail them out, like our new president. The best is yet to come.

I understand my grandfather owned some land, but he owed some tax he didn't know about until it got so high he didn't have money to pay it. He tried to borrow it from the bank with no luck, which probably was the plan from the get-go. The white man wanted the land, and that was a way to get it. He's not the only black person who lost land. They would buy this land with trees on it, clean it up, and as soon as it was in shape to plant on, the white man who wanted it would find a way to get it back. In 1964, this black man had some land, and this white man owned some land surrounding his. Everything was OK until this white man sold his land to another white man. This new white guy wanted to buy this black guy's land, but he didn't want to sell. This white guy told him that if he didn't sell his land to him, he was going to build up around his land to where he could not get in and out of his land, so he didn't have any choice but to sell.

Juneteenth is finally a holiday—it's been a *long* time coming. All happy days back in the sixties, when Sam Cooke sang: "It been a long time coming, but I know a change is going to come." I didn't understand what he was talking about back then; I thought he was just singing for the money or because he knew he had the best voice for singing I ever heard. Now I know what he was talking about. He knew something the rest of us didn't know. To you young black people who are working at these fast-food places and grocery stores, why don't you go to trade school or business school? I am sure you can do better, and money for that purpose is available. Contact your senator or congressperson—I am sure they can help you. Stop worrying about what you think the white man is doing to you and imagine what you can do for yourself. When I was young and trying to quit my bad habits, I would sing, "Things I used to do, I am not going to do no more." Now I sing, "Things I used to do, I can't do no more." I used to try to pimp, but women told me my head was too big. These men with small heads are, I guess, why the idea of man being addicted to sex probably was created by a lawyer, and men just use it to try to justify a bad behavior. Most of these addictions are just in a person's mind.

When are black people going to get the respect they earned? Black people saved this nation four times: during slavery, during the Revolutionary War, during the Civil War, and in the 2020 election. In all three wars, they were promised that when the war was over, they would be free, but as soon as the war was over, they were given back to their slave masters. I wonder: Will they ever meet any of their slaves in the next life? If so, I would like to hear what their slave masters would say to them to try to justify how they treated them, like whipping them for looking at a white woman or cutting off an ear if they tried to escape. Except the first time, if they got caught, if the master was in a bad mood, they might hang them. All the time, meanwhile, the white man was sleeping with these black women and girls.

If you people in Washington, D.C., cannot decide how to pay reparations to black people for slavery part one or slavery part two or whatever, I have a good idea. Pay the black people who were born before the Civil Rights Act passed in cash, and also give a payment to the children whose parents were born before the Civil Rights Bill and are now deceased whose birth certificate says Negro, colored, black, or African American. You all can decide what else needs to be done to try to atone for the sin of slavery. People ask me what I would do with the money. I couldn't care less about any money myself; I stopped drinking, I stopped smoking, and I stopped gambling. I am eighty years old, too old to go by the cathouse. All I want for myself is for the white man to apologize to black people for over four hundred years of mistreatment and appreciate what black people did for the richness of this country.

I was a member of this credit union one time, and when I got up to the window, this white lady asked me, "How can you be so happy? Every time you come in here, you are speaking and laughing." I said, "It's because I don't have any money to worry about!" I guess she was surprised to see a poor black man that happy. Another reason I am happy is that every morning when I rise, I look in the mirror, and I can see love all in my eyes. That lets me know there's got to be some God somewhere. Another time I went to the credit union, the same lady was there when I got up to the window. I asked her, "Can I ask you a question?" She said, "Shoot," and everybody in the building looked over there. She started laughing, and she said that was probably not a good thing to say in a bank.

I will be willing to bet that when black people begin to get reparations, some white people will be wearing afro wigs and getting a tan, saying they are black. That might be something, to see a white man walking around wearing an afro wig on his head if money is involved. The white man would be black only until he got the money. There are two laws, one for white people and one for black people, but that line that separates the black people from the white people is getting closer. One day we will cross that line. George Wallace hated black people, and he did *everything* he could to hurt black people, but before he died, he apologized to black people for his bad behavior and for the way he treated them. That let me know there is hope for the white people who think like Wallace did.

Every time I go in the bank to make a deposit, the tellers say, "How you doing, Mr. Goodloe?" and when I leave, they say, "You have a good day, Mr. Goodloe, and you come back and see us." I think about what happened to this guy I used to work with. They treated him the same way when he had about $80,000 in the bank, but he began to use drugs, and in about six months, he lost his new car, he lost his house, his wife left him, and he lost his job for stealing. One day he went back to the bank to get some money, and they told him, "Brown, all your money is gone. You owe us." After all his money was gone, he wasn't *Mr.* Brown anymore. He was just brown. Like when someone calls me trying to sell me something, they call me Mr. Henry or Mr. Goodloe, but when I owe them, they call me Henry or Goodloe or some other choice names. If white people are getting this COVID-19 vaccination, it must be safe, or at least they believe it's safe. That's why I got mine. The way some of these politicians are lying reminds me of this saying: "What's the use of telling the truth when a lie will do?" Some people believe a lie before the truth because it's less painful. Some people say the truth don't hurt, but that's a big fat lie.

When I lived in Detroit, I was at this service station, buying some gas, and this black guy came in there about half drunk. He told this guy that worked there, who was from another country, that back in the day white people used to call us nigger and coon. He asked this guy, "Over there, what did you all call us?" and this guy said the same thing. I worked with this guy from another country, and he told me not to trust men from that country. He said in the United States, people teach their kids to read and write, but he said that over there, that country was so poor that people teach their kids how to be slick so they can do better in life. When I lived in Detroit, one day I went in this store, shopping, and when I paid for what I bought, this guy gave me a $3 bill for my change like he thought I had just arrived in the United States on a boat. In Michigan, there is no tax on food. I bought some milk, and this guy charged me tax. I told him there was no tax on food, and he told me milk wasn't food. These guys from another country own a food store in Detroit, and they got busted for getting food from Focus Hope and taking it to their store and selling it. They would get these big bags of rice and put it in small sandwich bags and sell it, and black people would buy it when they could have gone to Focus Hope and gotten it for free.

My guess is that the only thing some white people care about Juneteenth for is that they get a day off from work with pay to get drunk. I hear some people say that if black people obeyed police when police stopped them, they might not get shot. The reason some people don't obey is that they might not hear what the police say because that loud music has damaged their hearing. One day my niece was playing her music loud, and I asked her who sang that song. She said, "I don't know." "What's the name of it?" "I don't know." "What are they saying, and why do you have it so loud?" "Because everybody else is doing it." I said, "I don't play my music loud," and she said, "You don't count." I guess I am too old to be hip. When I lived in Texas, this guy next door, I could always tell when he was going or coming when he got in his car. He would turn that music up so loud the windows on my apartment would be rattling. One day I was asleep, dreaming about this pretty lady movie star—I am not going to say who she was or what I asked her; use your imagination. Anyway, before I could get her answer, this guy woke me up with that loud music. I got mad, and when he left, I tried to go back to sleep and catch up with my dream. I could not. Then I was really mad. When he came back, I heard him coming, and I was standing in the door of my apartment, waiting on him. When he got there, I asked, "Do you got to play that music so loud?" He said, "It's just music." I said, "You think you so cool now, but about twenty or thirty years from now, when you can't hear, you are not going to think you are cool when you are walking around with hearing aids upside your head." I scared that guy straight—I never heard his loud music again.

The person next door to where I live now, I asked him for two years to turn his music down, but my words fell on deaf ears. One day he was playing that music loud in his car; he had all four doors open, and he was standing in the front door of his house. I was standing in the door of my house, and he saw a police car coming up the streets. I guess he thought I had called the police because he ran out to his car and turned down the music. When the police went by, this guy turned off the music, looked at me, and went in the house. I found out that day that he knew better because the next day he saw me he said, "Hey, friend." Five years later, he's still playing that music loud.

I've got "Black Lives Matter" on the back glass of my truck. This white guy saw it, and he said to me, "All lives matter." I told him, "You are talking to the wrong person. You should be talking to your friends because if everybody thought all lives matter, slavery never would have happened, and black people would not have been treated like second-class citizens for four hundred years." Let me talk about how the system works: When black people and poor white people were abusing drugs and dying, nobody seemed to care. But as soon as rich white people began to abuse drugs and started dying, suddenly, people cared. When people ask me who I trust the most, the Democrats or Republicans, I say neither. They ask if I vote, and I say yes. If you don't trust either party, why do you vote? I say because I can vote for who I think is the best of the two evils. Neither party is worth what the owl left in the nest after they ate. A president should have signed an executive order for reparations by now.

When people ask me what offends me, I say, "Nothing. I got thick skin like an alligator." When I grew up, we were playing the dozen. You had to be able to take it or get into a fight. One day me and this guy were playing the dozen, and he got mad. We got to fighting, and I didn't know he was left-handed. I was watching his right hand, but he put out my lights with his left hand. Back then, some of those guys had big, ashy fists. They could take a knife and scrape the skin off their fists like scales off a fish, and they could hit hard. Back then, if we had a disagreement, we didn't need no gun. We used our fists. We grew up to be real *men*. When we got grown, we still used our fists, and when it was over, we would laugh about who won and drink together. Back then, we were drinking that Thunderbird wine. We could get a fifth for sixty cents. Sometimes it took three or four of us to come up with sixty cents, but it seemed like the one who had the least money or no money would drink the most. There was a commercial about that wine: "What's the word? Thunderbird! What's the price? Thirty twice. Who drink the most? Negroes."

When we were growing up, one day it was raining, and I and two of my brothers were running up and down the road, playing in the rain. Momma came out on the porch and told us to come out of the rain and stay on the porch. We did, but as soon as she went back in the house, we went back to running up and down the road in that rain. All at once, there was a loud clap of thunder, and a bolt of lightning came rolling down the road and went past us. We took off running, but my youngest brother had just learned how to walk, so he tried to run and fell down. We ran off and left. Momma heard him crying, and she went and got him. When Momma made it back, we were sitting on the porch, and she said, "I bet you all will keep your ass on the porch now. I always told you all a hard head makes soft ass."

Another day, me and two of my brothers (the younger ones again) were picking up some pecans when we saw a skunk about fifteen yards from us. My younger brother picked up a rock, and before we could say "don't," he threw that rock at that skunk. That skunk turned around and raised his tail and sprayed that scent at us. It hit us. When we got home, we smelled so bad. Momma asked us what happened, and we told her. She said, "You all take off them clothes and take a bath." We did, but we didn't smell any better. Momma said, "You all didn't wash up good enough. Take another bath." We did, and that made us smell worse. Momma told us, "You all go outside, take these clothing with you, dig a hole in the backyard, and bury them." We did and went back in the house, but we smelled so bad Momma said, "You all go outside and play." We had that whole house smelling like a skunk, and it took about two weeks for that scent to wear off. The pecans we had picked up, we had to throw away because they smelled like skunk too.

One Saturday, Daddy, I, and my brother had to go to the woods to cut some firewood. Daddy told my brother, the same one that threw at that skunk, to get this mule and plow the garden. He asked his friend to help him, but neither one knew anything about plowing with a mule. They were in the pasture, and this man that lived close to the pasture saw them, and he went to see what they were doing. They were putting the collar on the mule upside down, and that man said, "That collar is upside down. What is they teaching you all in school?" My brother said, "They don't teach us about no stinking-ass mules in school!" One night daddy went hunting, and he shined his light up in a tree. He saw a raccoon, so he shot up there, and the coon fell on the ground. Daddy thought we was dead, so he put him in his hunting coat. When he got home, he reached into his coat to get the coon, and Daddy hollered so loud everybody in the house woke up. That coon scratched his hand and took some skin off it. One day one of my sisters and her friend went somewhere, and on the way back home, they saw this blue racer snake. These snakes have two feet back there by their tail, and they stand straight up like a person. The girls began to run, and this snake took off behind them. When they got to the house, they were sweating and out of breath. Daddy asked what was wrong, and they told him. Daddy said, "That snake was just playing with you all. That snake will run after you as long as you run. If you stop, they will stop; if you dance, they will dance; if you run at them, they will run."

I've heard some people say there's nothing sadder than a glass of wine alone. Wrong. Drink the whole bottle and wake up the next day with a hangover and broke. I know—I've been there. One of my brothers woke up one morning, and some dents were in his trailer. He didn't know how they got there, but what happened was, a tornado came through, so powerful it knocked a train off the track, and my brother never even woke up. Some people say we need more police; we just need good police, like in Windsor, Canada. When I lived in Detroit, I went over there for over twenty years, and I only ever saw one police car driving down the street. I had this talking fish hanging on the wall in my house. One night I walked in the house, and that fish started talking, and I got so frightened I started sweating. I took the battery out of that fish. This guy who owned a tackle store had a talking fish like that inside, on the wall by the door. Someone kicked in the door, trying to break in, and that fish started talking, and he took off running. He was seen on video, running down the street. The store owner said that fish was better security than the security system he had.

This woman saw some white smoke coming from airplanes, and she said it was something the white folks were spraying to kill black people. I said it would kill the white people too, but she said the white people had a town underground to live in, and she was for real. This other man had a horse, and he had trained it to bite people. One day he asked me and one of my brothers to help him do some work, and when we got there, he tried to make that horse bite us. That was funny to him until his shoe came untied, and he bent over to tie it, and that horse bit him in the rear end. We started laughing, and he got mad and told us to go home. Momma asked why we were back so soon, so we told her. A week later, he asked us to help him do that work again, but Momma told him we were busy.

This other woman was running for the union committee, so she gave some of us T-shirts saying so. This old guy said she didn't give him one, so I said, "She might want to give you something else—use your imagination." He said, "I can't do nothing with that, but I can wear the T-shirt." These two young kids were playing cowboy and crook. The one who was the cowboy caught the one who was the crook. He tied his hands behind him, put a rope around his neck, stood him up on a bucket, and kicked the bucket from under him—almost hung him. When he was asked why he did that, he said he had seen it on TV. This other kid was watching a cowboy movie on TV where the crook was getting the best of the cowboy. This guy got a gun and shot the crook through the TV.

One of my brothers was going with this woman from Louisiana. I sprayed some white ant killer in his yard, and when he got home from work, he saw it. He asked our other brother if he'd seen anybody hanging around his house. He said he'd seen some white powder by his house, and he thought somebody was trying to voodoo him. I found out that people from Alabama can lie. People from Arkansas talk trash. In Mississippi, they think they are bad. People from Tennessee think they are great lovers. Texas people think they look good. And people from Louisiana, everybody is afraid of, because they think they all know voodoo.

I heard this woman tell her child, "I'll be glad when school starts so I can get rid of you." That's why some of these children are out of control. These women have these children and expect these teachers, ballplayers, and singers to raise them. Question:

How come when black people act a fool, they are called a thug, but when white people act a fool, they are mentally ill? This one guy who lived in the city killed a squirrel in his backyard. He tried to cook it, but he said the longer he boiled it, the tougher it got. We found these turtle eggs, and we tried to boil them, but the longer we boiled them, the harder they got. We put them on a brick and hit them with a hammer, and they would just pop up in the air. We couldn't crack them, so we used them to play baseball.

This one guy had a habit of speeding down the street and showing out on his motorcycle. One day he was speeding down the street, and this car pulled out in front of him. He hit this car, and his head went flying over the car without his body. This other guy was tearing down his old house and found $15,000 in the wall. The same guy was up in this tree sawing off limbs later. He must have been thinking about that $15,000 he found, because he cut off the limb he was sitting on and fell to the ground.

When I was working on this rice farm, one Friday I got paid, and the first stop was the liquor store. I was up all night drinking and gambling, and when I went to work Saturday, I got sleepy. I lay down in the rice field and went to sleep. Something woke me up crawling across my belly—it was a big snake. I knocked it off and went back to sleep. I said, "When I get off work, I am going home and going to bed," but when I got off, the first stop was the liquor store again. I didn't go to bed until Sunday morning. The last time I took a drink was on a Friday in 1982. It made me so sick I stayed in bed until Monday evening, when I had to go to work. All that time, I didn't eat, drink water, or use the bathroom. I stayed sick for about a week. The last time I smoked a cigarette was in 1994. Things got so bad that when I breathed, it sounded like I was snoring, and I wasn't asleep. One thing about it: these things will warn you before they kill you. If you don't think you have the willpower to quit, ask God to give it to you. All you need is faith.

I put some flour in a small piece of plastic and mailed it to Tom Cotton. When the FBI interviewed me, they asked me: Did I have a mental problem? Was I in the army? Did I suffer from PTSD? I said no to all, but when I went to court, the judge told me if I wanted to see a mental illness doctor, they would pay for it. Those white people thought I was crazy. I moved from Arkansas to Detroit in 1966. In 1969, I came back on vacation. I walked in this store, and this white lady said, "Can I help you, sir?" I looked back because I thought a white guy had walked in behind me, but she was calling *me* sir, and that was the first time a white person had called me sir.

One of my nieces from Detroit was with me, and there's no tax on food in Michigan. She bought a cake, and the price said $1, but when she paid for it the lady said $1.03. When we got outside, my niece said, "I ought to jack that lady up. That cake said one dollar, and she charged me $1.03." I said three cents was for tax, and she said there was no tax on food. I said in Arkansas there is. The phone company owed me a refund. When I called them, that lady put me on hold for one hour and forty-five minutes. When she came back, she said, "I thought you had hung up by now." She didn't know I was watching Monday Night Football, Dallas and Washington, and had her on speaker. It was a toll call—that was back in 1980, when there was real football.

I heard a Republican politician say the forefathers thought slavery was necessary to save this union. He might be right, just like I am right about how black people are due reparations for saving this union. When people ask me if I think black people will ever be treated as equal, I say, "Yes, when Jesus comes back." If Trump would say he's Jesus, some people would believe him.

This guy broke in my house and stole a gun and some quarters. I told this lady about it, and she said it was her brother because he had a bunch of quarters. She said I should have him arrested. I said, "That's OK, he will get what's coming." A few days later, this lady was in bed when she heard window glass break. She got her pistol, sat in her rocking chair, and began to rock. That guy walked in her bedroom, saw that pistol, and turned to run, but she shot him in his rear end. When the police got there, he was on the ground moaning. The police said they were not going to arrest him because they believed he had learned his lesson. That guy began going to church after that.

This other guy robbed a bank: said he had a gun, got the money, and then sat down in the bank. The police asked him why he got the money and did not leave, and that guy just said it was because he was broke. They took him to a mental hospital. The police also saw this car riding low in the back, and when they stopped it, there was a trunk full of weed. They took the weed and let the guy go. They said, "Whoever's weed that was, that probably was their whole year's crop. When they miss their weed and kill that guy, we will arrest them!"

This guy's wife left him and took his kids and dog. He told me I should talk to the young people, but I said, "These young people don't listen to their elders. They think they know everything, but some of them can't tell a hog rotter from his tooter." I was trying to tell this young man how the sixties changed the course of history in the United States, and he said he knew all about the sixties. He had been all around the world, and he was born in 1960. Some of these lazy-ass politicians don't always look for the best way to solve a problem. They look for the easy way, like welfare. That created more problems than it solved. Like back in the day, about 90 percent of the people who were on welfare were young, healthy people who were able to work, but they chose welfare instead because it paid more than working. Detroit, Michigan, was the welfare capital of the world. One thing about these politicians: they don't care about giving away money as long as it don't come out of their own pockets.

When I was growing up, there were these shoes called penny loafers. They had an opening across the top where you could put a penny. We young people would put a piece of mirror in there and walk up to young women and talk to them. Every now and then, we would look down at that mirror and try to see under their dress. I tried that one day, and this young woman saw me. She hit me between the eyes so hard that for about a minute, I didn't see nothing but stars flashing in front of my eyes.

My guess is the reason some of these white people are mad is because they are poor and don't have any excuse for it. Some of these white people are singing the songs that black people sang back in the fifties. I heard this white guy singing one of them; it went: "If you ever been mistreated, you know what I am talking about. I worked five long years for one woman, and she had the nerve to put me out." He sounded like that happened to him for real.

This one guy was taking care of business with this woman up the side of the house. The next day, he was hurting and bleeding. He told this woman's mother, and she said, "Don't tell me; tell her!" He told her, and she said, "You wasn't doing it to me; you was doing it up against that rough tar paper on the house!" That same guy was going with a married woman. He went nuts over this woman, and this fool told her husband, "You better treat walking your wife right." That was the end of that love affair.

I was walking on the walking trail by the lake, and this woman was walking, doing something with her phone and not watching where she was going. She almost walked out into that lake. Another time, I was driving down the street and this woman was doing something with her phone, not watching where she was going, and walked in front of me. I almost hit her. This dog attempted to attack this guy, but that guy hit that dog with his fist and killed him. It's amazing how strong you are when you are frightened. This guy stole a car and was driving down the street. The police saw him, so they began to chase him. He sped up going across the overpass, and he lost control of the car and went over the rail, landing on the expressway. The car rolled over a few times, and when it ended up on its tires, that guy got out of the car and ran down the expressway. When he came up on the exit, the police were waiting for him. This guy robbed a bank on his lunch break, and he had on a shirt with his name and where he worked. When he got back to work, the police were there at his job. This other guy had some cows missing, and he paid these guys to help look for them. He found them at the stockyard and found out the guys he paid to help look for them were the ones who stole them.

This guy was at Daddy's house, and Daddy said he was going to see if his sweet potatoes were ready to dig, even though some of the vines didn't have potatoes on them. This guy had a way to dig potatoes and leave the vine. He and Daddy laughed about it, and Daddy said he'd never seen nothing like that before. This preacher was preaching one Sunday, and he told the senior citizens of his church, "Don't get mad at these young people for what they do; the only reason some of you are not doing it is because you done got too old." This lawyer said, "Don't be too hard on this policeman that killed Floyd, because he is the product of a broken system." Well, hell, I've been living in a broken system for seventy-nine years, plus I never killed anyone! For a person to kill Floyd the way he did, he must not have a heart—just a hole where his heart used to be.

This guy went into the store to buy a pop, and when the store owner told him the price, this guy said he thought a pop was still a dime. The store owner said that was fifty years ago. Some people don't want to die young, but they don't want to get old. All I can say is God bless your soul. This white woman worked at the post office, and she would bring this dog to work and put it on the counter. It would smell and lick people, and they wouldn't say nothing. One day, Momma went in there, and that dog attempted to do her the same way. Momma told that woman, "You better get that stinking-ass dog away from me." After that, every time Momma would go to the post office, that woman would put that dog on the floor. This black guy was on TV and said if black people were going to be in the sun, they should wear suntan lotion year-round if they didn't want to get skin cancer. I don't know where he comes from, but when we were young, we would work in the sun ten and eleven hours a day and never got skin cancer.

Some people wonder why white people are marching with Black Lives Matter people. They better march because if police keep killing black people and getting away with it, they are going to begin to kill poor white people next. The prettiest sight I have ever seen is out in the country at night: no lights, a blue sky full of stars, and a full moon shining. This one lady had a cat, and when it used the bathroom in the house she would whip it. One day when she was whipping that cat, it ran up her leg under her dress. She was jumping up and down shaking her dress, trying to get that cat from under her dress. Some people ask me why I don't have a dog. The only time I had a dog was back in the sixties.

When I was hunting for food, these two squirrels were in the yard. One would go around the house, get a pecan, come back, and put it in the ground. Then this other squirrel would dig it up and put it somewhere else. The first squirrel came back and caught him, and he made a noise and took off after this squirrel. They ran up the tree and down, and that squirrel chased that other squirrel around in the yard until he had enough. Then it made a sound and went back to pick up pecans and put them in the ground. That squirrel didn't mess with them again. This dog next door was in the yard, and a rabbit came from around the house. That dog saw it and began to run from it. It used to be the other way around—the rabbit would run from the dog. This guy went to prison, and when he got out, he said it was too hard out here, so he was going to do something to go back to prison. He was working at this place, and the owner knew him and where he lived. He robbed this place with a gun, went home, and sat on the porch waiting for the police to come get him. His mother told him he wasn't her son any more. While he was in jail, he took his belt and hung himself.

One Sunday this preacher was preaching, and he told the senior citizens, "Don't get mad at these young people for what they do; some of you used to do the same thing, and the reason you don't do it now is you done got too old." One Sunday the deacons weren't at church, so Momma asked the preacher, "Where are your jackass deacons?" This guy, when he was young, his nickname was Fox. He became a preacher, and one Sunday in church, Momma called him Fox. He said, "Don't call me Fox while we are in church. When we are not in church, you can call me anything." Momma said, "You better be glad I didn't call you a jackass!" Momma would tell us to do something, and if we didn't move fast enough, Momma would say, "Don't just stand there like the house by the side of the road!"

These people can't find workers, but if they hire Mexicans, then people will say they are taking our jobs. Somebody was stealing Daddy's chickens. One night he heard them, so he got his shotgun and went outside. When this guy saw him, he picked up a chicken and ran. Daddy shot at him, not to hit him but just to scare him. That guy dropped that chicken and turned on the jets. Daddy said he didn't know a white person could run that fast. He didn't steal any more of Daddy's chickens. One day I was driving down the expressway when this lady passed me. She had a piece of chicken in one hand, a biscuit in the other hand, and her knees on the steering wheel.

One day I was speeding, and the police stopped me. He said, "Do you know you were driving over the speed limit?" I said, "Yes, I call myself looking out for you, and I wasn't intending to get caught." He said, "I fooled you, didn't I?" He gave me a warning and told me to slow down. This one guy and some other cars were speeding down the expressway, but he was behind. The police stopped him, and he said, "Why didn't you stop the cars that were driving faster than me?" The police said, "You were easier to catch!" This other guy ran a red light, but he saw a police car, so he went backward through the light. The police stopped him and said, "I am not giving you a ticket for running the light but for backing up through the light." This guy from another country got stopped by the police. The police were talking to him, and this guy said, "Me no speak English." The police said, "If you don't speak English, you should not be driving, because you don't have any driving license, so I got to take you to jail." This guy said, "I was just joking! I can speak English." These people who can't speak good English, when they curse or say anything about money, you can understand them just fine. I haven't chopped or picked cotton for fifty-plus years, but I still dream about it and wake up hot and sweating. We went to visit the African American museum, and I was nice and cool. All at once, I got hot and began to sweat. I looked down, and I was standing over a picture of cotton painted on the floor.

When these women accuse these men of sexual harassment, I believe them. I worked with these white guys, and they would walk up behind each other and grab their ass, until one day one grabbed my ass. I broke his hand with a hammer I had in my hand. The boss said, "You didn't have to break his hand; he was just playing." I said, "I don't play like that. If you want him to feel somebody's ass, let him feel your fat ass." If these guys will grab a man's ass, imagine what they will do around a woman. This lady was at my house, and she said, "You must be gay." I said, "No, why?" She said, "You keep a cleaner house then most women!" She didn't believe I wasn't gay, so she and her girlfriend made a bet. The loser would find out if I was gay. She lost. Guess what she did to find out if I was gay? Use your imagination. Another woman told me, "You must be gay; I've never seen you with a woman." I told her what Daddy told us: never let your left hand know what your right hand is doing. You will be better off that way. Question: How come if I commit adultery, it's a sin, but if a preacher commits adultery, it's just poor judgment?

When people ask me how I can be so happy with all the problems that are going on, I tell them it's because I know when Jesus fixes it, everything is going to be all right. Another reason is that every morning when I rise, I look in the mirror, and I can see love all in my eyes; that lets me know there's got to be a God somewhere. This white guy was buying some land to build a town for white people only. He went on this talk show and said he was 100 percent white, but he took the test and found out he was 20 percent black. There's a saying: if you catch a sucker, bump their head. Looks like some people found plenty of suckers. They are telling all these lies to raise plenty of money.

When people ask me if I'm afraid that I might make somebody angry with what I am writing, I say, "I really don't care. I paid my dues to the United States. I don't owe anybody anything, except Jesus and myself." When I was young, I could pee up my nose; now when I pee, I pee on my toes. This black guy in Detroit opened up a store, so I tried to support him. I went there and bought something, and when I paid for it, I gave him a $20 bill. The first thing he said was, "You got anything smaller? You're going to take all my change. Can you go to the store across the street and get some change and come back?" I said OK, but he said, "Never mind, but you're going to take all my change." I said to myself, the way this guy thinks, he's not going to make it. In about six months, he was out of business. I went grocery shopping, and this black lady checked me out. I gave her a $100 bill, and she said, "You got anything smaller? You're going to take all my change." Lady, the white people own this store—they've got plenty of change in the office.

This guy in Detroit opened up a business selling home security systems. On his business windows, he had iron bars. In about six months, he was out of business. When I was growing up, we had this bed headboard made of iron. We would jump over it, but the last time I tried it, I didn't make it over it—I sat down on it. Every man knows how painful that was. I worked with this guy in the factory, and his wife bought him a watch that cost $250. For some reason, that watch wouldn't run inside that factory. I had a watch that cost $9, and it would run in the factory. That guy said, "What kind of shit is this?"

I worked with these two guys driving tractors on the farm. They were going to make their own beer, but they drank some before it aged long enough. It tore up their stomachs. Every time they began driving and the tractor bounced up and down, they had to stop and use the toilet. These white people that are doing all that talking and lying and showing off their guns are trying to get black and white people mad at each other and start a race war. If it happened, they would be the first to run and hide, like at the capitol. If the people were on friendly tours like some people say, why didn't they go greet them and talk to them? That's what a real man with balls would have done. Trump promised to meet them at the capitol, but he got in his bulletproof car and went the other way, and some people are still falling for his bull. When President Obama invited Trump to the White House, it looked like he was as afraid to be around a black man as a long-tail cat in a room full of rocking chairs.

When violence happens like what happened at the capitol, and people say that's not who we are, that *is* who we are. This country was built on violence, beginning with slavery and the two wars that happened in America. If you live by the sword, you die by the sword. If we don't get our act together and respect each other, all I can say is God have mercy on us all.

President Biden and Vice President Harris, there needs to be a program set up to pay black people reparations for slavery part one and slavery part two, which began in 1865, the same year part one ended. To help fund the program, these ballplayers and others that come to the U.S. and make all that money income-tax-free should pay into the program instead of taking all that money back to their country. People from other countries come to the U.S. and pimp off black people, getting the money we should be getting for reparations. White people, God is watching you all. Like I said, judgment day is coming: Will you be ready? We all got a debt to pay in the end, no credit or excuses or exceptions. Will your debt be paid to black people for the sin of slavery? These people who say the election was stolen are just as bad as me if I get caught sitting up sleeping, and I say I wasn't asleep. I had my eyes closed, checking for cracks in my eyelids. When people tell me I don't look to be as old as I am, I tell them ugly people don't age fast; they just get uglier. This black guy told me he wanted to sing to make a living. I told him if he tried to sing, he wasn't going to make it. White folks sing like Frank Sinatra and Bing Crosby; black folk *sang* like Sam Cooke and Johnnie Taylor.

There was a white sheriff in Altheimer, Arkansas. He was hard on black people. This black guy was taking a dip of snuff on the street, and the sheriff arrested him and took him to jail and said he was drinking. This sheriff owned a liquor store, and he would sit down the street. When a black person would buy some liquor and come out of the store, he would arrest them and take the liquor back to the store and resell it. He made this black guy his deputy, and this black guy arrested a white guy. The sheriff told him, "I didn't want you to arrest white people; I wanted you to arrest the niggers," and he fired him. This sheriff went to arrest this black guy, and this guy shot the sheriff's hat off his head. The sheriff fell down and played dead. The sheriff told his friends, "I believe if I hadn't played dead, this nigger was going to kill me!" The sheriff tried to get the state police to go arrest this black guy, but they said no to his request. The governor of Arkansas advised this black guy to leave Arkansas, and he said he could not guarantee his safety.

If black people don't get reparations for slavery part one or slavery part two, which began in 1865, the same year that slavery part one ended, I don't see one reason black people should keep voting. As much as black people did for the richness of this country for little or no pay, we deserve better. I voted for Obama, but he did more for poor white people who didn't vote for him than he did for me. He got them health insurance, something I've had since 1967. Why is it that Jewish people got reparations for the Holocaust, Hawaii got reparations for the bombing of Pearl Harbor, and Native Americans got reparations? Why can't black people get reparations? Correct me if I am wrong, but I heard the Catholic church owned slaves. I am sure in a hundred-and-fifty-some years a president could have signed an executive order for reparations. These peoples who say the election was rigged: they know better. That's not why they are angry. They are angry because they are poor and don't have any good reason for being that way. My guess is that some of them ended up poor because they spent their time trying to make black people's lives worse instead of trying to make their own life better.

I am going to keep on walking in God's name for peace all over this world. In Jesus's name, God put a song in my heart. I am going to keep on singing, yes I am. I am sometimes up; I am sometimes down. God saw some good in me, and he let me stay around. I feel great! I wouldn't take nothing for my journey home; when I leave this world, I can't take money alone. I feel great! You can talk about heaven night and day, but in the end you got a price to pay. I feel great! Some people don't want to die young, but they don't want to get old; all I can say is God bless your soul. I feel great! I would rather die on my feet than live on my knees. If you can't hear, read my lips, please. I feel great! If you think you are at the end of your rope, trust in God: there is always hope. I feel great early in the morning; I feel great late in the evening; I feel great in the midnight hour; I feel great! Take the weight off my shoulder and let me do my thing. Treat me like I am a rich white man. I feel great! If the white man had to go through what I been through, I wonder what would he do? I feel great! Jesus died on the cross so our souls won't be lost. I feel great! I am going to keep on walking in God's name; I believe that will make me a better man. I feel great! When I was growing up, I used to wish I was white; now I know that wasn't right. I feel great! You can talk about me night and day; the more you talk, the more I am going to pray. I feel great! Things I used to do, I don't do no more. Judgment day is coming—God said so. I feel great! I could have been dead and in the ground; God saw some good in me and let me stay around. I feel great! One day I won't have to think about war no more; Jesus is coming back! He said so. I feel great! When my way gets dark and I can't see, God sends his love and rescues me. I feel great! I am sometimes right; I am sometimes wrong; I am going to keep on praying until I reach my heavenly home. I feel great! I was born in a world of sin; I believe God will be with me in the end. I feel great! It might not rain for forty days and forty nights, but when Jesus comes back everything is going to be all right. I feel great! At the end of the road, when I've done my best, I am going home to be at rest. I feel great! Thank God, I feel great! Thank Jesus, I feel great.

9 798822 935075